MAR        2007

W9-ALE-242
6 1524 00462 1894

J
599.4        Preszler, June,
Pre              1954-

              Bats.

WITHDRAWN
Woodridge Public Library

| DATE | | | |
|---|---|---|---|
| APR 1 8 2007 | | AUG 1 3 2007 | |
| MAY 2 3 2007 JUN 0 9 2007 | | OCT 2 9 2007 | |
| | | AUG 1 2008 | |
| JUL 2 4 2007 | | | |
| JUL 3 1 2007 | | | |
| | | | |

WOODRIDGE PUBLIC LIBRARY
3 PLAZA DRIVE
WOODRIDGE, IL 60517-5014
(630) 964-7899

BAKER & TAYLOR

World of Mammals

# Bats

by June Preszler

Consultant:
Barbara French, Conservation Specialist
Bat Conservation International
Austin, Texas

Capstone
press

Mankato, Minnesota

WOODRIDGE PUBLIC LIBRARY
3 PLAZA DRIVE
WOODRIDGE, IL 60517-5014
(630) 964-7899

Bridgestone Books are published by Capstone Press,
151 Good Counsel Drive, P.O. Box 669, Mankato, Minnesota 56002.
www.capstonepress.com

Copyright © 2006 by Capstone Press. All rights reserved.
No part of this publication may be reproduced in whole or in part, or stored in a retrieval
system, or transmitted in any form or by any means, electronic, mechanical, photocopying,
recording, or otherwise, without written permission of the publisher.
For information regarding permission, write to Capstone Press,
151 Good Counsel Drive, P.O. Box 669, Dept. R, Mankato, Minnesota 56002.
Printed in the United States of America

*Library of Congress Cataloging-in-Publication Data*
Preszler, June, 1954–
    Bats / by June Preszler.
      p. cm.—(Bridgestone books. World of mammals)
    Includes bibliographical references and index.
    ISBN-13: 978-0-7368-5415-3 (hardcover)
    ISBN-10: 0-7368-5415-0 (hardcover)
    1. Bats—Juvenile literature. I. Title. II. World of mammals.
QL737.C5P74 2006
599.4—dc22                                                          2005019867

Summary: A brief introduction to bats, discussing their characteristics, range, food, offspring, and dangers.
    Includes a range map, life cycle diagram, and amazing facts.

**Editorial Credits**
Katy Kudela, editor; Molly Nei, set designer; Kim Brown and Patrick D. Dentinger, book designers;
    Wanda Winch, photo researcher; Scott Thoms, photo editor; Tami Collins, life cycle illustrator;
    Nancy Steers, map illustrator

**Photo Credits**
Bat Conservation International/Dr. Merlin D. Tuttle, 4, 6, 10, 12, 16, 20
Digital Vision/NatPhotos, 1
Getty Images Inc./National Geographic/Tim Laman, 18
McDonald Wildlife Photography/Joe McDonald, cover

1 2 3 4 5 6 11 10 09 08 07 06

# Table of Contents

# Bats

Bats are creatures of the night. As the sun sets, these dark-winged animals fly from their **roosts**. They swoop through the sky in search of food.

Although they can fly, bats are not birds. Bats belong to a group of animals called **mammals**. Mammals have backbones and fur. Female mammals feed milk to their young.

Bats make up one quarter of all mammals in the world. There are more than 1,100 bat **species**.

◄ Bats are the only mammals that can fly.

# What Bats Look Like

Bats have furry bodies. Some bats are brown, black, or gray. Other bats have red, yellow, or white fur.

Bats have four long fingers and a curved thumb. Stretchy skin covers the fingers to form wings. Bats use their feet to hang from roosts.

Bats come in many sizes. The world's smallest bat is the hog-nosed bat. Its wings stretch only 6 inches (15 centimeters). Some bats grow much larger. The flying fox bat has a **wingspan** of up to 6 feet (2 meters).

◄ The hog-nosed bat weighs less than a penny. It is often called the bumblebee bat because it is so small.

# Bat Range Map

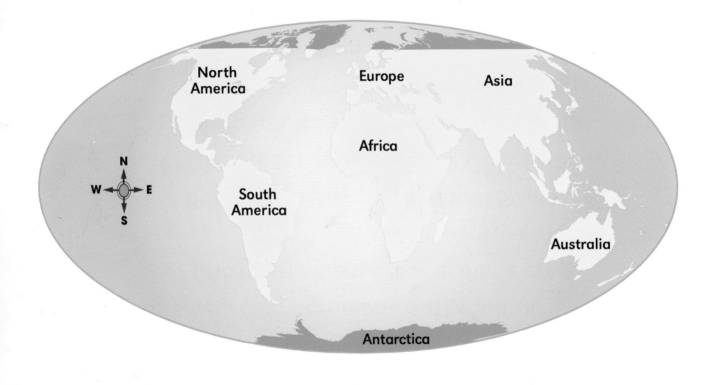

North America · Europe · Asia · Africa · South America · Australia · Antarctica

N · W · E · S

Where Bats Live

# Bats in the World

Two groups of bats live in the world. Most bats are microbats. These small bats live throughout the world, except in polar areas. Bats known as megabats are generally larger in size. They live only in tropical areas.

# Bat Habitats

Bats are **nocturnal** animals. They sleep during the day and hunt at night.

These daytime sleepers look for dark, quiet places to rest. They like old empty buildings and caves. They squeeze into the cracks of bridges. Bats also find shelter in trees and attics.

Millions of bats can live together in one **colony**. These bats flock to the same roost. They crowd together for warmth and safety.

◀ To keep warm, these young pallid bats roost close together under a bridge.

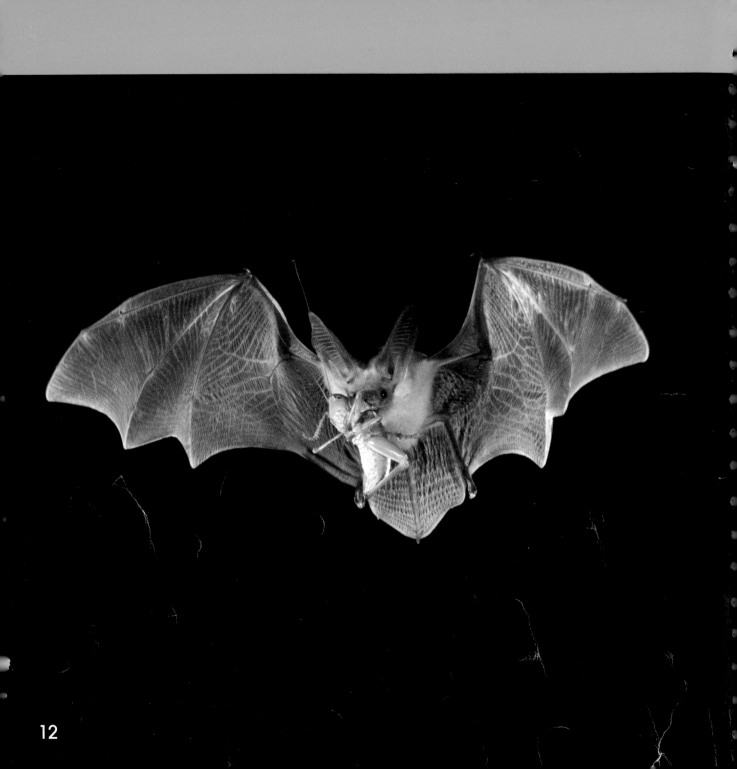

# What Bats Eat

Each species of bat has its own diet. Megabats and some microbats eat fruit, flowers, and leaves. Some bats use their long tongues to drink **nectar** from flowers. Most microbats feed on insects. Some catch fish, frogs, and other small animals.

Vampire bats have the most unusual diet. They feed on blood. These bats gently land on an animal. They cut their **prey** with their front teeth, then lap the blood with their tongues.

◀ A pallid bat catches a grasshopper by surprise. The pallid bat is one of many bats that feeds on insects.

# The Life Cycle of a Bat

Newborn pup

3-week-old pup

Adult male
and female

# Producing Young

Depending on the species, bats **mate** in the fall, winter, or spring. A single male bat can mate with 30 or more females. Some males attract females by singing screechy notes.

Most female bats have only one pup a year. They often join other female bats in a roost to give birth and to raise their pups.

Pups are born into the world helpless. Their eyes are closed at birth. They have no fur on their bodies. Pups cling to their mothers for safety.

## Growing Up

Bat pups grow quickly. They open their eyes just a few days after birth. Most pups drink their mother's milk for the first few weeks. Then they learn to fly and hunt for food.

Bats live longer than most other small mammals. Some bats can live 30 years or more.

◄ A fruit bat pup huddles underneath its mother's wings for warmth.

# Dangers to Bats

Humans are the greatest danger to bats. Some people fear bats and try to destroy them. Other people change bat habitats with buildings and construction projects.

Many people do not know how helpful bats can be. Bats eat a lot of insects that damage crops and bother people. They also spread pollen and seeds to help plants grow.

All bats are in danger of dying out. But some organizations are trying to save these night creatures. They teach people about bats. They also work to save bat habitats.

◀ A man tries to free a bat from a mist net, used to collect water. People didn't know the nets would affect wildlife.

# Amazing Facts about Bats

- Some bats, such as the vampire bat, can walk, run, and jump.
- A bat can eat 1,200 mosquito-sized insects in an hour.
- Microbats call out high-pitched sounds. These sounds bounce off objects and return to the bats as echoes. Echoes help microbats find insects to eat.
- Bats don't usually attack humans. But like most wild animals, bats will bite if touched. Wildlife experts advise people to leave bats alone.

◄ A vampire bat can tiptoe quietly towards its prey.

# Glossary

colony (KOL-uh-nee)—a group of animals that live together in the same area

mammal (MAM-uhl)—a warm-blooded animal that has fur and a backbone

mate (MAYT)—to join together to produce young

nectar (NEK-tur)—a sweet liquid in flowers

nocturnal (nok-TUR-nuhl)—to be active at night

prey (PRAY)—an animal hunted by another animal for food

roost (ROOST)—a place where a bat rests and sleeps

species (SPEE-sheez)—a group of animals or plants that share common characteristics

wingspan (WING-span)—the distance between the outer tips of the wings of a bat

# Read More

**Heinrichs, Ann.** *Bats.* Nature's Friends. Minneapolis: Compass Point Books, 2004.

**Raabe, Emily.** *Vampire Bats.* The Library of Bats. New York: PowerKids Press, 2003.

# Internet Sites

FactHound offers a safe, fun way to find Internet sites related to this book. All of the sites on FactHound have been researched by our staff.

Here's how:

1. Visit *www.facthound.com*

2. Type in this special code **0736854150** for age-appropriate sites. Or enter a search word related to this book for a more general search.

3. Click on the **Fetch It** button.

FactHound will fetch the best sites for you!

# Index